Every Part of This Earth Is Sacred

Every Part of This Earth Is Sacred

Native American Voices in Praise of Nature

Edited by Jana Stone *Photographs by* Mel Curtis *and* Bonnie Sharpe

HarperSanFrancisco
A Division of HarperCollinsPublishers

Permissions acknowledgments appear on pages 134–37.

EVERY PART OF THIS EARTH IS SACRED: *Native American Voices in Praise of Nature.*
Copyright © 1993 by StoneWork Editions. Photographs copyright © 1993 by Mel Curtis and
Bonnie Sharpe. All rights reserved. Printed in Hong Kong. No part of this book may be used or
reproduced in any manner whatsoever without written permission except in the case of brief
quotations embodied in critical articles and reviews. For information address HarperCollins
Publishers, 10 East 53rd Street, New York, NY 10022.

Produced by StoneWork Editions
Creative Direction: Jana Stone and Mel Curtis
Design: Ann Amberg and Sarah Conradt

FIRST EDITION

Library of Congress Cataloging-in-Publication Data

Every part of this earth is sacred: Native American voices in praise of nature /
edited by Jana Stone ; photographs by Mel Curtis and Bonnie Sharpe. — 1st ed.
    p.   cm.
    Includes bibliographical references.
    ISBN 0-06-250848-2 (alk. paper)
    1. Indians of North America — Philosophy. 2. Indians of North
    America — Religion and mythology. 3. Human ecology — North America.
    I. Stone, Jana. II. Curtis, Mel. III. Sharpe, Bonnie.
    E98.P5E94 1993   92-43415
    304.2'08997073 — dc20   CIP

    93 94 95 96 97 HCHK 10 9 8 7 6 5 4 3 2 1

This edition is printed on acid-free paper that meets the American National Standards
Institute Z39.48 Standard.

He loved the earth and all things of the earth. . . . He knew that man's heart away from nature becomes hard; he knew the lack of respect for growing, living things soon led to the lack of respect for humans too.

LUTHER STANDING BEAR | *Oglala Sioux*

CONTENTS

PREFACE

For so many of us searching for ways to regain balance in our relationship with the earth, the traditional ways of Native America offer wise counsel and guidance. Within the ancient rhythms and patterns of these traditions, we are finding the possibilities for living in grace and harmony with nature.

These pages celebrate and honor those traditions. Images of quiet beauty and rich color illustrate a chorus of tribal voices. First, with lyrical verse that includes Chippewa song, Zuni offering, and Winnebago meditation, "This Newly Created World" pays homage to the Native American reverence for the earth, water, and sky. Then, to document the consequences of non-Indian mistreatment and destruction of lands once rich in life and beauty, "The White Man Does Not Understand" cites the memories of the Omaha, Nez Perce, and Duwamish tribes and recalls the protests of such great leaders as Black Hawk, Tecumseh, and Sitting Bull. And finally, through the thoughtful reflections of a Cayuse warrior, a Sioux chief, and a Stoney elder, the ceremonial chants of the Navajo and Ojibwa prayers of thanksgiving, "The Great Spirit's Book Is the Whole of Creation" reveals the sacred spirit that inhabits the earth and informs our connection to all of creation.

Consider the wisdom of these words from Young Chief of the Cayuse, "The ground says, The Great Spirit has placed me here to produce all that grows on me, trees and fruit. The same way the ground says, It was from me that man was made. The Great Spirit, in placing men on earth, desired them to take good care of the ground and to do each other no harm." If we accept and act on this vision of our place within nature, then we, too, may come to live wisely and responsibly on the earth.

THIS NEWLY CREATED WORLD

Earth

Water

Sky

The earth has been laid down, the earth has been laid down

The earth has been laid down, it has been made.

The earth spirit has been laid down

It is covered over with growing things, it has been laid down

The earth has been laid down, it has been made.

The sky has been set up, the sky has been set up

The sky has been set up, it has been made.

The mountains have been laid down, they have been made.

The mountain spirits have been laid down

They are covered over with all the animals, they have been laid down

The mountains have been laid down, they have been made.

The waters have been laid down, the waters have been laid down

The waters have been laid down, they have been made.

The water spirits have been laid down

They are covered over with the water pollen, they have been laid down

The waters have been laid down, they have been made.

The clouds have been set up, the clouds have been set up

The clouds have been set up, the clouds have been made.

SWEATHOUSE CHANT | *Navajo*

Pleasant it looked,

this newly created world.

Along the entire length and breadth

of the earth, our grandmother,

extended the green reflection

of her covering

and the escaping odors

were pleasant to inhale.

THIS NEWLY CREATED WORLD

Winnebago

Holy Mother Earth, the trees and all nature

are witnesses of your thoughts and deeds.

MEDITATION | *Winnebago*

That our earth mother may wrap herself

In a fourfold robe of white meal;

That she may be covered with frost flowers;

That yonder on all the mossy mountains

The forests may huddle together with the cold;

That their arms may be broken by the snow,

in order that the land may be thus,

I have made my prayer sticks into living beings.

OFFERING | *Zuni*

as my eyes

look over the prairie

I feel the summer in the spring

SPRING SONG | *Chippewa*

In summer the rains come and the grass comes up.

That is the time that the deer has new horns.

SONG | *Yaqui*

The great sea

Has sent me adrift

It moves me

As the weed in a great river

Earth and the great weather

Move me

Have carried me away

And move my inward parts with joy.

UVAVNUK | *Eskimo*

Close to the west the great ocean is singing.

The waves are rolling toward me, covered with many clouds.

Even here I catch the sound.

The earth is shaking beneath me and I hear the deep rumbling.

RAIN SONG | *Papago*

From the half

Of the sky

That which lives there

Is coming, and makes a noise.

THE APPROACH OF THE STORM
<hr>
Ojibwa

You, whose day it is, make it beautiful.

Get out your rainbow colors,

So it will be beautiful.

SONG TO BRING FAIR WEATHER

Nootka

This Newly Created World

37

All living creatures and all plants derive their life from the sun. If it were not for the sun, there would be darkness and nothing could grow — the earth would be without life. If the sun alone were to act upon animals and plants, the heat would be so great that they would die, but there are clouds that bring rain, and the actions of the sun and earth together supply the moisture that is needed for life. . . . This is according to the laws of nature.

OKUTE | *Teton Sioux*

here am I

behold me

I am the sun

behold me.

SUNRISE GREETING │ *Lakota Sioux*

THE WHITE MAN DOES NOT UNDERSTAND

Our Land Is More Valuable Than Your Money

It Will Last Forever

Many years ago when our grandparents foresaw what our future would be like, they spoke their prophecies among themselves and passed them on to the children before them:

"Cities will progress and then decay to the ways of the lowest beings. Drinkers of dark liquids will come upon the land, speaking nonsense and filth. Then the end shall be near.

"Population will increase until the land can hold no more. The tribes of men will mix. The dark liquids they drink will cause the people to fight among themselves. Families will break up: father against children and the children against one another.

"Maybe when the people have outdone themselves, then maybe, the stars will fall upon the land, or drops of hot water will rain upon the earth. Or the land will turn under. Or our father, the sun, will not rise to start the day. Then our possessions will turn into beasts and devour us whole.

"If not, there will be an odor from gases, which will fill the air we breathe, and the end for us shall come.

"But the people themselves will bring upon themselves what they receive. From what has resulted, time alone will tell what the future holds for us."

PROPHECY | *Zuni*

The White Man Does Not Understand

49

We always had plenty; our children never cried from hunger, neither were our people in want. . . . The rapids of Rock River furnished us with an abundance of excellent fish, and the land being very fertile, never failed to produce good crops of corn, beans, pumpkins, and squashes. . . . Our village was healthy and there was no place in the country possessing such advantages, nor hunting grounds better than those we had in possession. If a prophet had come to our village in those days and told us that the things were to take place which have since come to pass, none of our people would have believed them.

BLACK HAWK | *Sac and Fox*

When I was a youth the country was very
beautiful. Along the rivers were belts of timberland,
where grew cottonwood, maple, elm, ash, hickory,
and walnut trees, and many other shrubs. And
under these grew many herbs and beautiful
flowering plants.

In both the woodland and the prairies I
could see the trails of many kinds of animals and
could hear the cheerful songs of many kinds of
birds. When I walked abroad I could see many
forms of life, beautiful living creatures which
Wakanda had placed here; and these were, after
their manner, walking, flying, leaping, running,
playing all about.

But now the face of all the land is
changed and sad. The living creatures are gone. I
see the land desolate and I suffer an unspeakable
sadness. Sometimes I wake in the night and feel as
though I should suffocate from the pressure of this
awful feeling of loneliness.

ANONYMOUS | *Omaha*

The White people never cared for land or bear. When we Indians kill meat, we eat it all up. When we dig roots we make little holes. When we build houses, we make little holes. When we burn grass for grasshoppers, we don't ruin things. We shake down acorns and pinenuts. We don't chop down the trees. We only use dead wood. But the White people plow up the ground, pull down the trees, kill everything. The tree says, "Don't. I am sore. Don't hurt me." But they chop it down and cut it up. The spirit of the land hates them. The Indian never hurts anything, but the White people destroy all. They blast rocks and scatter them on the ground. The rock says, "Don't. You are hurting me." But the White people pay no attention. When the Indians use rocks, they take little round ones for their cooking. . . . How can the spirit of the earth like the White man? . . . Everywhere the White man has touched it, it is sore.

ANONYMOUS HOLY WOMAN | *Wintu*

You ask me to plow the ground. Shall I take a knife and tear my mother's breast? Then when I die she will not take me to her bosom to rest.

You ask me to dig for stone. Shall I dig under her skin for her bones? Then when I die I cannot enter her body to be born again.

You ask me to cut grass and make hay and sell it and be rich like the white man. But how dare I cut off my mother's hair?

SMOHALLA | *Nez Perce*

I wish all to know that I do not propose to sell any part of my country, nor will I have the whites cutting our timber along the rivers, more especially the oak. I am particularly fond of the little groves of oak trees. I love to look at them, because they endure the wintry storm and the summer's heat, and — not unlike ourselves — seem to flourish by them.

SITTING BULL | *Sioux*

The earth was created by the assistance of the sun, and it should be left as it was. . . . The earth and myself are of one mind. The measure of the land and the measure of our bodies are the same. . . . Understand me fully with reference to my affection for the land. I never said the land was mine to do with it as I chose. The one who has the right to dispose of it is the one who created it.

CHIEF JOSEPH | *Nez Perce*

EVERY PART OF THIS EARTH IS SACRED

No tribe has the right
to sell, even to each other, much
less strangers. . . . *Sell a country!*
Why not sell the air, the great sea,
as well as the earth! Did not the
Great Spirit make them all for the
use of his children?

TECUMSEH | *Shawnee*

Of course, none but an adoring one could dance for days with his face to the sacred sun, and that time is all but done. We cannot have back the days of the buffalo and beaver; we cannot win back our clean blood-stream and superb health, and we can never again expect the beautiful rapport we once had with Nature. The springs and lakes have dried and the mountains are bare of forests. The plow has changed the face of the world. *Wi-wila* is dead! No more may we heal our sick and comfort our dying with a strength founded on faith, for even the animals now fear us, and fear supplants faith.

LUTHER STANDING BEAR | *Oglala Sioux*

The earth is our mother. The white man is ruining our mother. I don't know the white man's ways, but to us the Mesa, the air, the water, are Holy Elements. We pray to these Holy Elements in order for our people to flourish and perpetuate the well-being of each generation. . . .

The whites have neglected and misused the Earth. Soon the Navajo will resemble the Anasazi ruins. The wind took them away because they misused the Earth.

The white men wish that nothing will be left to us after this is over. They want us like the Anasazi.

Who likes it, nobody likes it, everybody has something to do with it. Our Mother is being scarred.

ASA BAZHONOODAH | *Navajo*

The white man does not understand the Indian for the reason that he does not understand America. He is too far removed from its formative processes. The roots of the tree of his life have not yet grasped the rock and soil. The white man is still troubled by primitive fears; he still has in his consciousness the perils of this frontier continent, some of its vastnesses not yet having yielded to his questing footsteps and inquiring eyes. He shudders still with the memory of the loss of his forefathers upon its scorching deserts and forbidding mountain-tops. The man from Europe is still a foreigner and an alien. And he still hates the man who questioned his path across the continent.

But in the Indian spirit the land is still vested; it will be until other men are able to divine and meet its rhythm. Men must be born and reborn to belong. Their bodies must be formed of the dust of their forefathers' bones.

LUTHER STANDING BEAR | *Oglala Sioux*

Every part of this soil is sacred in the estimation of my people. Every hillside, every valley, every plain and grove, has been hallowed by some sad or happy event in days long vanished. The very dust upon which you now stand responds more lovingly to their footsteps than to yours, because it is rich with the blood of our ancestors and our bare feet are conscious of the sympathetic touch. Even the little children who lived here and rejoiced here for a brief season will love these somber solitudes and at eventide they greet shadowy returning spirits. And when the last Red Man shall have perished, and the memory of my tribe shall have become a myth among the White Men, these shores will swarm with the invisible dead of my tribe, and when your children's children think themselves alone in the field, the store, the shop, upon the highway, or in the silence of the pathless woods, they will not be alone. At night when the streets of your cities and villages are silent and you think them deserted, they will throng with the returning hosts that once filled and still love this beautiful land. The White Man will never be alone.

CHIEF SEALTH | *Duwamish*

The Great Spirit's Book Is the Whole of Creation

All Is Beautiful

All Around Me

Grandfather,

Look at our brokenness.

We know that in all creation
Only the human family
Has strayed from the Sacred Way.

We know that we are the ones
Who are divided
And we are the ones
Who must come back together
To walk in the Sacred Way.

Grandfather,
Sacred One,
Teach us love, compassion, and honor
That we may heal the earth
And heal each other.

PRAYER | *Ojibwa*

Hills are always more beautiful than stone buildings, you know. Living in a city is an artificial existence. Lots of people hardly ever feel real soil under their feet, see plants grow except in flowerpots, or get far enough beyond the street light to catch the enchantment of a night sky studded with stars. When people live far from the scenes of the Great Spirit's making, it's easy for them to forget his laws.

WALKING BUFFALO | *Stoney*

We should understand well that all things are the works of the Great Spirit. We should know that He is within all things; the trees, the grasses, the rivers, the mountains and all the four-legged animals, and the winged peoples; and even more important we should understand that He is also above all these things and peoples. When we do understand all this deeply in our hearts, then we will fear, and love, and know the Great Spirit, and then we will be able to act and live as He intends.

BLACK ELK | *Sioux*

We saw the Great Spirit's work in almost everything: sun, moon, trees, wind, and mountains. Sometimes we approached him through these things. Was that so bad? . . . Indians living close to nature and nature's ruler are not living in darkness.

WALKING BUFFALO | *Stoney*

The man who sat on the ground in his tipi meditating
on life and its meaning, accepting the kinship of all creatures
and acknowledging unity with the universe of things was
infusing into his being the true essence of civilization.

LUTHER STANDING BEAR | *Oglala Sioux*

When I was ten years of age I looked at the land and the rivers, the sky above, and the animals around me and could not fail to realize that they were made by some great power. I was so anxious to understand this power that I questioned the trees and the bushes: "Who made you?" I looked at the moss covered stones; some of them seemed to have the features of a man, but they could not answer me. Then I had a dream, and in my dream one of these small round stones appeared to me and told me that the maker of all was *Wakan tanka*, and that in order to honor him I must honor his works in nature.

BRAVE BUFFALO | *Sioux*

I wonder if the ground has anything to say? I wonder if the ground is listening to what is said? I wonder if the ground would come alive and what is on it? Though I hear what the ground says. The ground says, It is the Great Spirit that placed me here. . . . The ground, water and grass say, The Great Spirit has given us our names. We have these names and hold these names. The ground says, The Great Spirit has placed me here to produce all that grows on me, trees and fruit. The same way the ground says, It was from me man was made. The Great Spirit, in placing men on earth, desired them to take good care of the ground and to do each other no harm.

YOUNG CHIEF | *Cayuse*

This covers it all,

The Earth and the Most High Power Whose Ways Are Beautiful.

All is beautiful before me,

All is beautiful behind me,

All is beautiful below me,

All is beautiful all around me.

This covers it all,

The Skies and the Most High Power Whose Ways Are Beautiful.

All is beautiful.

CHANT | *Navajo*

The Lakota was a true naturalist — a lover of nature. He loved the earth and all things of the earth, the attachment growing with age. The old people came literally to love the soil and they sat or reclined on the ground with a feeling of being close to a mothering power. It was good for the skin to touch the earth and the old people liked to remove their moccasins and walk with bare feet on the sacred earth. . . . The soil was soothing, strengthening, cleansing and healing. . . . Kinship with all creatures of the earth, sky, and water was a real and active principle. For the animal and bird world there existed a brotherly feeling that kept the Lakota safe among them and so close did some of the Lakota come to their feathered and furred friends that in true brother-hood they spoke a common tongue.

The old Lakota was wise. He knew that man's heart away from nature becomes hard; he knew the lack of respect for growing, living things soon led to lack of respect for humans too. So he kept his youth close to its softening influence.

LUTHER STANDING BEAR | *Oglala Sioux*

Behold, my brothers, the spring has come; the earth has received the embraces of the sun and we shall soon see the results of that love!

Every seed has awakened and so has all animal life. It is through this mysterious power that we too have our being and we therefore yield to our neighbors, even our animal neighbors, the same right as ourselves, to inhabit this land.

SITTING BULL | *Sioux*

I turn to the Great Spirit's book which is the whole of his creation. You can read a big part of that book if you study nature. You know, if you take all your books, lay them out under the sun, and let the snow and rain and insects work on them for a while, there will be nothing left. But the Great Spirit has provided you and me with an opportunity for study in nature's university, the forests, the rivers, the mountains, and the animals which include us.

WALKING BUFFALO | *Stoney*

The Great Spirit's Book Is the Whole of Creation

The Great Spirit's Book Is the Whole of Creation

117

We return thanks to our mother, the earth, which sustains us. We return thanks to the rivers and streams, which supply us with water. We return thanks to all herbs, which furnish medicines for the cure of our diseases. We return thanks to the corn, and to her sisters, the beans and squashes, which give us life. We return thanks to the bushes and trees, which provide us with fruit. We return thanks to the wind, which moving the air, has banished diseases. We return thanks to the moon and stars, which have given us their light when the sun was gone. We return thanks to our grandfather *He-no*, that he has protected his grandchildren from witches and reptiles, and has given us his rain. We return thanks to the sun, that he has looked upon the earth with a beneficent eye. Lastly, we return thanks to the Great Spirit, in whom is embodied all goodness, and who directs all things for the good of his children.

PRAYER | *Iroquois*

Remember, remember the sacredness of things

running streams and dwellings

the young within the nest

a hearth for sacred fire

the holy flame of fire

SONG | *Pawnee · Osage · Omaha*

Tsegihi.

House made of dawn,

House made of evening light,

House made of dark cloud,

House made of male rain,

House made of dark mist,

House made of female rain,

House made of pollen,

House made of grasshoppers,

Dark cloud is at the door.

The trail out of it is dark cloud.

The zigzag lightning stands high upon it.

Male deity!

Your offering I make.

I have prepared a smoke for you.

Restore my feet for me,

Restore my legs for me,

Restore my body for me,

Restore my mind for me,

Restore my voice for me.

My interior feeling cool, may I walk.

No longer sore, may I walk.

Impervious to pain, may I walk.

With living feelings, may I walk.

As it used to be long ago, may I walk.

Happily may I walk.

Happily, with abundant dark clouds, may I walk.

Happily, with abundant showers, may I walk.

Happily, with abundant plants, may I walk.

Happily, on a trail of pollen, may I walk.

Happily may I walk.

Being as it used to be long ago, may I walk.

May it be beautiful before me,

May it be beautiful behind me,

May it be beautiful below me,

May it be beautiful above me.

May it be beautiful all around me.

In beauty it is finished.

BEAUTYWAY *from* NIGHT CHANT

Navajo

NATIVE AMERICAN TRIBES

CAYUSE Closely associated with the Nez Perce and Wallawalla, this Northwest tribe formerly occupied territory near the headwaters of the Wallawalla, Umatilla, and Grand Ronde rivers in Washington and Oregon. Their first contact with non-Indians came with the Lewis and Clark expedition in 1805, which was soon followed by the arrival of missionaries, hunters, and settlers. Though the Cayuse were considered especially warlike by white settlers, disease, not war, was what nearly destroyed the tribe in 1847 with an epidemic of smallpox. An 1855 treaty forced the Cayuse onto a reservation near Pendleton, Oregon, with the Wallawalla and Umatilla tribes.

CHIPPEWA /OJIBWA One of the largest tribal groups north of Mexico, the Chippewa/Ojibwa (To Roast Until Puckered Up) are an Eastern Woodlands and North Plains tribe of the Algonquian-Wakashan language group that also includes the Ottawa, Potawatomi, Cree, and Muskegon tribes. In the seventeenth century the Chippewa/Ojibwa occupied lands in the Great Lakes region from Lake Huron to Lake Superior and extending into Minnesota. Their first recorded contacts with Europeans were with French Jesuit missionaries in 1640. By the eighteenth century, the Chippewa had firearms which they used in wars against their traditional enemies the Sioux and the Fox, driving the Sioux westward across the Mississippi and the Fox south into an alliance with the Sac. The Chippewa, like all tribes in the Northwest territories, took part in resisting the frontier settlement of the region, but by 1815 those living within the United States had made a treaty with the government and subsequently resided on reservations or allotted lands in their traditional territories in Michigan, Wisconsin, Minnesota, and North Dakota.

DUWAMISH A small tribe of the Coast Salish, the Duwamish lived on the western shores of Washington's Puget Sound. The Coast Salish comprised several dozen hunter-gatherer tribes clustered along the abundant shores of the Northwest coast from the Columbia River to north of the Canadian border. All of the Coast Salish tribes share a proud cultural heritage especially noted for boldly carved art forms marked by environmental and spiritual symbolism. The Duwamish are most closely associated with another Coast Salish tribe, the Suquamish, because of Chief Sealth (Seattle), the son of a Duwamish father and a Suquamish mother. Through the 1855 Point Elliott Treaty, Chief Sealth ceded Coast Salish lands between Olympia, Washington, and the Canadian border to the United States government.

ESKIMO/INUIT These Arctic Circle coastal tribes are found from the Bering Sea to Greenland and northeastern Siberia. Especially skilled at adapting to the extreme Arctic climate, the Eskimo (Those Who Eat Their Food Raw) depend principally on sea mammals for food, clothing, oil, tools, and weapons. Though living in small, migrating bands, they share rich religious and mythological traditions that are revealed through beautifully carved soapstone, ivory, and bone sculpture.

IROQUOIS One of the greatest and most powerful alliances of Native American tribes, the Iroquois (We Who Are of the Extended Lodge) Confederacy or League was formed about 1570 when the great leader Hiawatha, a Mohawk, and his disciple Dekanawida brought together five Eastern Woodlands nations: the Mohawk (From the Land Where the Partridge Drums), the Oneida (A Boulder Standing Up), the Cayuga (Place Locust Were Taken Out), the Onondaga, and the Seneca (Place of the Stone). In 1722, the Tuscarora (Hemp Gatherers) joined what became the Six Nation Confederacy. By the end of the seventeenth century, at the height of their power, the Iroquois controlled a vast territory from western Massachusetts in the north to Ohio in the west; and from southern Canada to as far south as North Carolina. The Iroquois structure of intertribal republican governance with councils of elected delegates served as a model for the United States Constitution. Today the Iroquois are found primarily in New York, Wisconsin, Oklahoma, Ontario, and Quebec.

NAVAJO/DINEH The Navajo/Dineh (the People) are an Athapascan tribe originally from northwestern Canada who migrated to the American Southwest in the fourteenth century. This fierce nomadic tribe terrorized the more sedentary Pueblo tribes, who referred to them as *apachu*, enemy-strangers. The Navajo came to adopt many of the cultural practices of the Pueblos, including religious dance ceremonies, pottery making, and weaving. They became highly skilled silversmiths under the influence of the Spanish. With a current population of around 160,000 and more than sixteen million acres of reservation lands covering parts of Arizona, New Mexico, and Utah, the Navajo Nation is the largest Native American tribe in the United States. Mining the reservation's oil and mineral deposits in combination with sheep and cattle ranching has made the Navajo one of the wealthiest Indian nations in North America.

NEZ PERCE/SHAHAPTIAN The Nez Perce (French meaning pierced noses) are a Northwest tribe found in western Idaho, northeastern Oregon, and southeastern Washington. Their first contacts with whites came with the 1805 expedition of Lewis and Clark. By 1855, along with their neighboring tribes the Cayuse and the Wallawalla, the Nez Perce were forced to cede large parts of their territory to the United States government and were confined to a reservation that included parts of the Wallowa Valley of Oregon and a large part of western Idaho. The discovery of gold in the 1860s brought disputes with miners and non-Indian settlers over treaty-secured Nez Perce lands. Under the charismatic leadership of Chief Joseph, the Nez Perce fought back, but severe defeats at the hands of U.S. troops forced Joseph to attempt a retreat across the Canadian border. He was captured with a band of warriors within miles of the border. His eloquent surrender speech ends: "Hear me, my chiefs. I am tired: my heart is sick and sad. From where the sun now stands, I will fight no more forever." Contact with non-Indians proved disastrous. In 1805 the total population of the Nez Perce was about 6,000; by 1906 their population was reduced to only 1,600.

NOOTKA/WEST COAST This group of tribes lives on the west coast of Canada's Vancouver Island. First contact with Europeans came in the eighteenth century with the Pacific explorations of Captain James Cook, who imposed the name *Nootka*. Like the Coast Salish tribes to the south, the Nootka/West Coast tribes share a long tradition as great artists and carvers producing flowing, abstract, geometric carved interpretations of nature. It is this art that best articulates the West Coast perception of the oneness of all earth's creatures, human and animal.

OMAHA A southern branch of the western Sioux, the Omaha (Upstream People) were originally found on the Ohio and Wabash rivers, but were pushed northwest up the Mississippi and into present-day Iowa and Nebraska. In the mid-nineteenth century, the Omaha sold much of their land to the United States and after 1882 most members of the tribe owned land individually. Lewis and Clark encountered the Omaha in 1803, witnessing the Omaha's ceremonial powwow, *Whe'wahchee* or Dance of Thanksgiving, which is still observed annually.

OSAGE This southern Siouan tribe of the western division was first encountered in 1673 by French traders on the Osage River in Missouri. The Osage (*Wazhazhe*) Nation was once classed with the Omaha, Ponca, Kansa, and Quapaw, with whom they constituted a single body living along the lower Ohio River valley. By 1810, the Osage began ceding their lands in Missouri to the United States and were moved to reservations in Oklahoma. The discovery of oil on reservation lands has made the Osage Nation one of the wealthiest tribes in the United States.

PAPAGO The Papago (the Beans People) are a southwestern Piman tribe of the Uto-Aztecan language group whose traditional home was south and southeast of the Gila River from south of Tucson, Arizona, into northern Sonora, Mexico. Like their Pima neighbors, the Papago are descendents of the ancient Hohokam people. The Papago were subsistence desert farmers employing irrigation systems to raise maize, beans, and cotton. They suffered severe oppression at the hands of their traditional enemy, the nomadic Apache (Navajo), and the first non-Indian invaders, the Spanish. Today, most Papago are farmers and cattle raisers living on reservation lands near Tucson.

PAWNEE The Pawnee (*pariki*, horn) are a Great Plains tribe closely affiliated with the Caddo, Arikawa, and Wichita tribes. Calling themselves *Chahiksichahiks* (Men of Men), the Pawnee lived in earth lodges near the Platte and Republican rivers in present-day southern Nebraska. Known as fierce fighters, the Pawnee were traditional enemies of the Sioux and the Cheyenne. In the early eighteenth century they numbered 10,000, but epidemics and wars, primarily conducted against the Sioux, greatly reduced their numbers. Today there are 2,000, mostly living off the reservation in Oklahoma. The Pawnee enjoy a culture rich in elaborate myths and religious rituals. Every July, the four bands of the Pawnee — the Chaui or Grand Pawnee, the Kitkehahki or Republican Pawnee, the Pitahaurat or Tapage Pawnee, and the Skidi or Wolf Pawnee — come together for a powwow honoring the traditions of clan and tribal bonds.

SAC AND FOX The Sac (*Osa Kiwug*, People of the Yellow Earth) and the Fox (*Muskwakiwuk*, People of the Red Earth) were two separate, neighboring Eastern Woodlands tribes. Originally from the Great Lakes region, the Sac and Fox banded together in 1804 for protection and survival. A combination of Chippewa/Ojibwa aggression from the north and non-Indian settlers from the east pushed the Sac and Fox south into Illinois, Iowa, Missouri, and Kansas, and finally forced settlement in the Indian Territory in

1869. 1832 saw the last major Sac and Fox resistance to non-Indian settlements in war against the United States under the leadership of the great chief Black Hawk.

SHAWNEE An Eastern Woodlands tribe of the Algonquian language group, the Shawnee were originally from the area around the Savannah River in present-day North Carolina and the Cumberland Valley. Conflicts first with neighboring Cherokee and Catawba, then Iroquois and non-Indian settlers, caused them to move north and west to the Ohio River valley during the eighteenth century. Forced to move again in 1795, this time to Indiana, the Shawnee established a village on the Tippacanoe River. Though lead by one of the great Native American orators, Tecumseh, the Shawnee were unable to withstand attacks by U.S. troops led by William Henry Harrison and were finally badly defeated in 1811 with the total destruction of their village. Moving west first into the Kansas territory and finally to Oklahoma, the Shawnee were incorporated into the Cherokee Nation reservation in 1870.

SIOUX The Sioux are a Great Plains confederacy of tribes divided into eastern, southern, and western divisions from Hokan-Siouan stock. Before contact with non-Indians, the majority of Sioux, numbering close to 30,000, lived in an area extending from west of the Mississippi northward from the Arkansas River and west nearly to the Rocky Mountains. The nomadic western division, which included the Lakota, Teton, and Oglala tribes, calling themselves *Ikche-Wichasha* (the Real Natural Human Beings), were highly regarded as brilliant horsemen, buffalo hunters, and warriors. All through the nineteenth century, they resisted non-Indian incursions into their traditional tribal lands but by 1867 were driven onto a Dakota reservation. Gold found in the Black Hills brought invading white prospectors, who were met with resistance under the leadership of Sitting Bull, Red Cloud, and Crazy Horse. A final battle against U.S. troops came in 1890 with the massacre of 200 mostly unarmed women and children at Wounded Knee. In 1979, the Sioux Nation won a $105 million judgment in a suit begun in 1923 for the unlawful taking of their lands.

STONEY/ASSINIBOINE A Great Plains tribe of the Siouan language group, the Stoney/Assiniboine (One Who Cooks by the Use of Stones) traditionally lived along the Saskatchewan and Assiniboine rivers in Canada, and the upper Missouri River in present-day North Dakota and Montana. Though ethnically and linguistically related, they were allied against the Sioux with the Cree. Contact with non-Indians in the 1830s brought a smallpox epidemic that killed more than 4,000 of the tribe's estimated population of 10,000. Today a small number of Assiniboine live on reservations at Fort Belnap and Fort Peck, Montana.

WINNEBAGO An Eastern Woodlands tribe of Hokan-Siouan stock, the Winnebago (*Winipyagohagi*, People of the Dirty Water) traditional homelands were south of Green Bay in present-day Wisconsin. Their culture was built around worship of an elaborate pantheon of deities that were honored through ceremonies and dances: Earth Maker, Sun, Moon, Evening Star, Night Spirit, Thunderbird, and Great Rabbit. The Winnebago were among those tribes that suffered the greatest oppression from non-Indian settlers and the U.S. government. Between 1829 and 1866, the Winnebago were denied treaty-secured lands and forcibly moved seven times. Greatly reduced in number, they eventually settled on reservations in Nebraska and Wisconsin. Present-day Winnebagos number around 800, living primarily in Wisconsin.

WINTU A small California tribe, the Wintu (the People) were found in the valleys of the upper Sacramento and upper Trinity rivers and were closely related to the Wintun found on the west side of the Sacramento Valley from the river and up to the Coast Range. Disease and aggression from non-Indian settlers reduced the population from 12,000 in 1770 to just over 1,000 by 1910. By the 1930 census, the combined recorded population of the Wintu and Wintun tribes was only 512.

YAQUI A tribe or tribal division of the Cahita tribe of the Uto-Aztecan ethnic and linguistic family, the Yaqui are believed to have originally come to the American Southwest from the Rio Yaqui in north central Sonora, Mexico.

ZUNI The Zuni are a pueblo-dwelling tribe of the Aztec-Tanoan language group living in the Southwest. They were the first Pueblo tribe to be encountered by the Spanish in 1539. The following year Coronado, thinking he had found El Dorado, lay siege to the Zuni pueblo at Hawikuh. By 1692 the Zuni had fled to their last stronghold on top of an inaccessible mesa and built one single village on the site of the ancient pueblo of Halona. This site, about 30 miles south of Gallup, New Mexico, has remained the center of the Zuni nation. The Zuni are a sedentary farming tribe who honor their spiritual connection to the earth through a tradition of communal religious ceremonies, dances, and arts.

Text Sources and Acknowledgments

Epigraph

page 5 Luther Standing Bear, reprinted from *Land of the Spotted Eagle*, by Luther Standing Bear. Copyright © 1933 by Luther Standing Bear. Renewal copyright © 1960 by May Jones. Lincoln: University of Nebraska Press, 1978, pp. 192–97. Reprinted by permission of the University of Nebraska Press.

This Newly Created World

page 13 Sweathouse chant, from *Navajo Creation Myth,* by Hasteen Klah, recorded by Mary C. Wheelwright. Sante Fe: Museum of Navajo Ceremonial Art, 1942; reprinted by AMS, Inc., New York, pp. 136–37.

page 15 Winnebago song, from *The Road of Life and Death: A Ritual Drama of the American Indians,* by Paul Radin. Princeton: Princeton University Press, 1945, p. 254.

page 19 Winnebago meditation, from *Prairie Smoke,* by Melvin Randolph Gilmore. New York: Columbia University Press, 1929, p. 9.

page 21 Zuni offering, from "Introduction to Zuni Ceremonialism," by Ruth Bunzel. Washington, DC: Bureau of American Ethnology, 47th Annual Report, 1929–1930, pp. 483–84.

page 25 Chippewa song, from "Chippewa Music II," by Frances Densmore. Washington, DC: Bureau of American Ethnology, Bulletin 53, 1913, p. 254.

page 26 Yaqui song, from *Literature of the American Indian,* edited by Thomas E. Sanders and Walter W. Peek. Mission Hills, CA: Glencoe Press, 1973, 1976, p. 61.

page 29 Uvavnuk, from *Intellectual Life of the Iglulik Eskimos,* by Knut Rasmussen, translated from Danish by W. E. Calvert, 1930, p. 123.

page 33 Papago rain song, from *Literature of the American Indian,* Sanders and Peek, p. 59.

page 35 Ojibwa rain song, from *Literature of the American Indian*, Sanders and Peek, p. 59.

page 36 Nootka song, from *Literature of the American Indian*, Sanders and Peek, p. 48.

page 38 Okute, from "Teton Sioux Music," by Frances Densmore. Washington, DC: Bureau of American Ethnology, Bulletin 61, 1918, pp. 172–73.

page 41 Lakota sunrise song, reprinted from *The Spiritual Legacy of the American Indian*, by Joseph Epes Brown. Copyright © 1982 by Joseph Epes Brown. New York: Crossroad, 1982, p. 105. Reprinted by permission of The Crossroad Publishing Company.

THE WHITE MAN DOES NOT UNDERSTAND

page 47 Zuni prophecy, from *The Zunis: Self-Portrayals*, by the Zuni People. Albuquerque: University of New Mexico Press, 1972.

page 53 Black Hawk, from *Autobiography of Black Hawk as Dictated by Himself to Antoine LeClair*. Historical Society of Iowa, 1833; reprinted by American Publishing Company, Rock Island, IL, 1912, pp. 62–63.

page 54 Anonymous Omaha, from *Prairie Smoke*, Gilmore, p. 36.

page 57 Anonymous Wintu holy woman, from *Freedom and Culture*, by Dorothy Lee. Englewood Cliffs, NJ: Prentice-Hall, 1959, pp. 163–64. (Originally cited in *Religious Perspectives in College Teaching*, edited by Hoxie N. Fairchild, New York: John Wiley, 1952.)

page 63 Smohalla, 1850(?) speech, from *Biography and History of the Indians of North America*, 3rd ed., by Samuel G. Drake. Boston: O. L. Perkins and Hillard, Gray & Company, 1854, p. 27.

page 64 Sitting Bull, from *Sitting Bull, Champion of the Sioux*, by Stanley Vestal. Boston and New York: Houghton Mifflin, 1932, p. 97.

page 66 Chief Joseph, from *War Chief Joseph,* by Helen Addison Howard. Caldwell, ID: The Caxton Printers, 1941, p. 84.

page 69 Tecumseh, 1810 speech, from *The Portable North American Indian Reader,* edited by Frederick W. Turner III. Copyright © 1973, 1974 by The Viking Press, Inc. New York and London: Viking Penguin, 1977, p. 246. Used by permission of Viking Penguin, a division of Penguin Books USA Inc.

page 73 Luther Standing Bear, from *Land of the Spotted Eagle,* Standing Bear, p. 257.

page 75 Asa Bazhonoodah, from *Problems of Electrical Power Production in the Southwest,* Senate Hearings of Interior and Insular Affairs Committee, Pt. 5, May 28, 1971.

page 80 Luther Standing Bear, from *Land of the Spotted Eagle,* Standing Bear, p. 248.

page 83 Chief Sealth (Seattle), from 1851 speech. Seattle: Washington State Historical Society.

THE GREAT SPIRIT'S BOOK IS THE WHOLE OF CREATION

page 89 Ojibwa prayer, from *Earth Prayers,* edited by Elizabeth Roberts and Elias Amidon. Copyright © 1991 by Elizabeth Roberts and Elias Amidon. New York: HarperCollins, 1991, p. 95. Reprinted by permission of HarperCollins *Publishers.*

page 93 Walking Buffalo, from *Tatanga Mani, Walking Buffalo of the Stonies,* by Grant MacEwan. Edmonton, Alberta: M. J. Hurtig, 1969, p. 5. Reprinted by permission of the author.

page 94 Black Elk, from *The Sacred Pipe: Black Elk's Account of the Seven Rites of the Oglala Sioux,* edited by Joseph Epes Brown. Copyright © 1953 by the University of Oklahoma Press. Norman: University of Oklahoma Press, 1953, p. xx. Used by permission of the publisher.

page 97 Walking Buffalo, from *Tatanga Mani,* MacEwan, p. 181.

page 103 Luther Standing Bear, from *Land of the Spotted Eagle,* Standing Bear, p. 250.

page 104 Brave Buffalo, from "Teton Sioux Music," Densmore, pp. 207–8.

page 107 Young Chief, 1855 speech, from *The Indian Council in the Valley of the Walla Walla*, by Lawrence Kip, 1855, p. 22.

page 108 Navajo chant, from *Literature of the American Indian*, Sanders and Peek, p. 191.

page 112 Luther Standing Bear, from *Land of the Spotted Eagle*, Standing Bear, pp. 192–97.

page 115 Sitting Bull, 1877 speech, from *To Serve the Devil, Vol. I: Natives and Slaves,* by Paul Jacobs and Saul Landeau. New York: Vintage Books, 1971, pp. 3–4.

page 116 Walking Buffalo, from *Tatanga Mani,* MacEwan, p. 6.

page 119 Iroquois prayer, from *League of the Ho-de-no-sau-nee,* by Lewis Morgan, translated by Ely S. Parker, 1851, pp. 202–3.

page 123 Pawnee/Osage/Omaha song, from *Earth Prayers*, Roberts and Amidon, p. 196.

pages 124–25 Navajo chant, from *Literature of the American Indian*, Sanders and Peek, pp. 193–94.

PHOTOGRAPHY CREDITS

The Great Spirit's Book Is the Whole of Creation

About the Producers

Jana Stone, Editor Working in collaboration with artists, illustrators and designers, Ms. Stone develops and produces books through StoneWork Editions, a book packaging company specializing in inventive, fine-quality illustrated books. Most recently, Ms. Stone produced and edited the eight-book series *Belles Lettres*. Each book in the series illustrated the work of an individual writer on a single subject: Ralph Waldo Emerson, *Self-Reliance;* William Shakespeare, *Selected Sonnets*; Mark Twain, *The Adam and Eve Diaries*; Gertrude Jekyll, *Pleasure in a Garden*; Ambrose Bierce, *The Secret of Happiness and Other Fantastic Fables*; Robert Louis Stevenson, *Talk and Talkers*; Gertrude Stein, *Notes on Money*; and Henry David Thoreau, *Walking*.

Mel Curtis, Photographer A Seattle-based commercial and fine art photographer, Mr. Curtis's photographs illustrated Emerson's *Self-Reliance* for the *Belles Lettres* series. He is a graduate of the University of Cincinnati, the School of Design, Architecture and Art; and holds a masters degree in photography from Ohio University, the School of Art. His photographs are included in the permanent collection of the Corcoran Gallery of Art in Washington D.C. and the corporate art collections of Microsoft, IBM, AT&T, and the Gannett Company. This is his third book.

Bonnie Sharpe, Photographer A strong interest in the natural sciences led to Ms. Sharpe's choice of subject as an artist. She travels extensively, often for months at a time, in pursuit of beautiful images. She holds a degree in art history from the University of Wisconsin. This is her first book.

Ann Amberg, Senior Designer A 1983 graduate of the Colorado Institute of Art, Ms. Amberg is a graphic designer with a particular interest in Native American culture and its view of the environment. Currently working with a coalition of Northwest tribes, she is fighting to preserve Snoqualmie Falls in Washington, considered a sacred place by the region's native tribes.

Sarah Conradt, Designer Ms. Conradt is a graduate of the University of Washington, School of Art and Design.